J 973.311
Landa
Landau, Elaine.

Witness the Boston Tea
Party /

Witness the

Boston Tea Party

with Elaine Landau

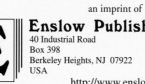

Enslow Elementary

an imprint of

Enslow Publishers, Inc.

40 Industrial Road   PO Box 38
Box 398   Aldershot
Berkeley Heights, NJ 07922 Hants GU12 6BP
USA   UK

http://www.enslow.com

For Hailey Louise Albers.

Enslow Elementary, an imprint of Enslow Publishers, Inc.

Enslow Elementary® is a registered trademark of Enslow Publishers, Inc.

Library of Congress Cataloging-in-Publication Data:

Landau, Elaine.
    Witness the Boston Tea Party with Elaine Landau / Elaine Landau.
       p. cm. — (Explore Colonial America with Elaine Landau)
    Includes bibliographical references and index.
    ISBN 0-7660-2553-5
    1. Boston Tea Party, 1773—Juvenile literature. I. Title. II. Series.
    E215.7.L36 2006
    973.3'115—dc22
                         2005008383

Printed in the United States of America

10 9 8 7 6 5 4 3 2 1

To Our Readers: We have done our best to make sure all Internet Addresses in this book were active and appropriate when we went to press. However, the author and the publisher have no control over and assume no liability for the material available on those Internet sites or on other Web sites they may link to. Any comments or suggestions can be sent by e-mail to comments@enslow.com or to the address on the back cover.

Series Literacy Consultant: Allan A. De Fina, Ph.D., Past President of the New Jersey Reading Association and Professor, Department of Literacy Education, New Jersey City University.

Illustration Credits: Clipart.com, p. 33; © Corel Corporation, pp. 12, 27 (top), 41 (bottom); David Pavelonis, Elaine & Max illustrations on pp. 1, 3, 4, 5, 6, 7, 11, 13, 17, 21, 22, 25, 29, 33, 34, 39, 42, 43; Centers of Military History, pp. 36, 44 (bottom); Elaine Landau, p. 43; Enslow Publishers, Inc., pp. 4–5, 16 (right), 18, 40; Hemera Technologies, Inc./Enslow Publishers, Inc, p. 2; Hemera Technologies, Inc./Enslow Publishers, Inc./Library of Congress, backgrounds on pp. 3–7, 43–48; © Jeff Greenberg/The Image Works, p. 38; Larry Allain, USGS, p. 13; Library of Congress, pp. 6, 7, 10, 14, 15, 19 (bottom), 20, 25 (second from top), 28 (bottom), 31, 32, 41 (top), 42; © Michael J. Doolittle/The Image Works, p. 23 (top); National Archives and Records Administration, p. 35 (bottom), 37; Old South Meeting House, p. 16 (left); Photo by Susan Wilson, www.susanwilsonphoto.com, pp. 23 (bottom), 24, 25 (top), 30; Reproduced from *The American Revolution: A Picture Sourcebook*, by John Grafton, Dover Publications, Inc., 1975, pp. 8, 9, 26, 28 (top), 35 (top), 39, 44 (top); Robinson half chest, part of the permanent collection of the Boston Tea Party Ship & Museum, pp. 1, 27 (bottom); © Topham/The Image Works, p. 19 (top).

Front Cover Illustrations: David Pavelonis (top); Time Life Pictures/Getty Images (bottom).

Back Cover Illustrations: David Pavelonis (Elaine & Max); Robinson half chest, part of the permanent collection of the Boston Tea Party Ship & Museum (Tea Chest).

Contents

BOSTON
MASSACHUSETTS
1773

KEY

= British Merchant Ship

→ = Route to Tea Party

★ = Site of Boston Tea Party

BEACON HILL

John Hancock's House

Old Granary Burying Ground

Boston Common

Common Burying Ground

ME
PART OF MA

NH

NY   MA   Boston

CT

RI

PA

New York City

Philadelphia   Trenton

MD

NJ

DE

VA

Atlantic Ocean

4

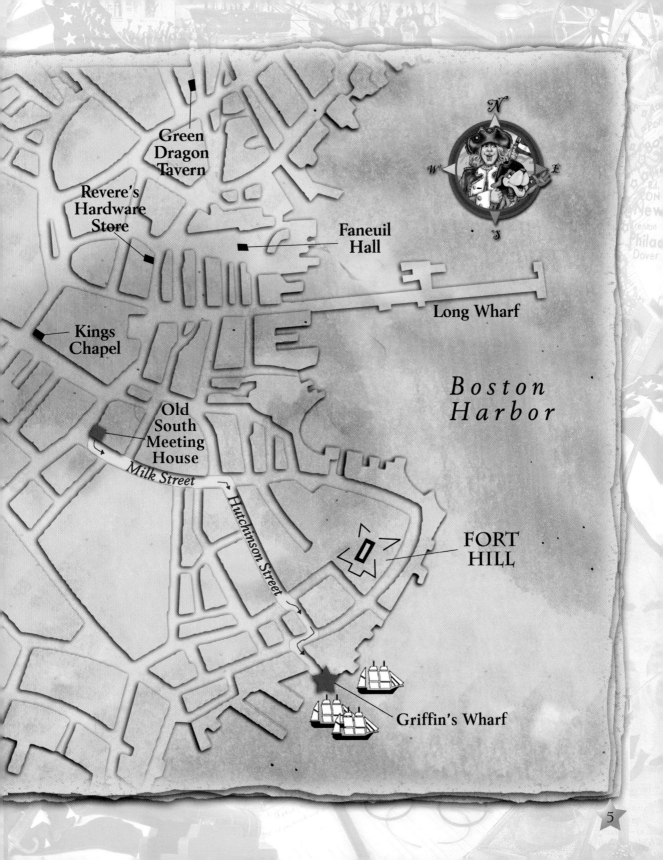

Green
Dragon
Tavern

Revere's
Hardware
Store

Faneuil
Hall

Kings
Chapel

Old
South
Meeting
House

Milk Street

Hutchinson Street

Long Wharf

*Boston
Harbor*

FORT
HILL

Griffin's Wharf

Dear Fellow Explorer,

What if you had a time machine? Imagine turning a dial to travel back in time. Where would you go? Would you head for colonial times? That could be exciting. You could help build a new nation.

Picture being in Boston, Massachusetts, on December 16, 1773. That was when the Boston Tea Party took place. Of course, it was not a real party. That chilly night the colonists stood up to Britain.

The Boston Tea Party of 1773

Their actions changed life in the colonies for good.

I am Elaine Landau and this is my dog, Max. Max and I do quite a bit of time traveling. We are going to the Boston Tea Party. The trip was Max's idea. He is a very **patriotic** pooch.

Come along with us. There is a lot to see. Use this book as your time machine. It will take you back to colonial Boston with us. Are you ready to takeoff? Okay. Fasten your seat belt. Then blast off by turning the page.

The Boston Tea Party was one of the events leading up to the American Revolution.

GRIFFIN'S WHARF IS THIS WAY, MAX.

I CAN'T WAIT TO GET THERE. THAT'S WHERE THE BOSTON TEA PARTY OCCURRED!

1 How It All Began

It was almost the winter of 1773. Trouble had been brewing in the Massachusetts **colony** for months. The colonists were upset. They felt that they were being treated unfairly and wanted to put a stop to it. They were angry at King George III of Britain and **Parliament** (the British government). The problem had to do with taxes.

At the time, Britain needed money. It had recently finished fighting a long war against France in both Europe and the colonies. Now it had to pay for the cost of the war. Britain hoped to raise the money by taxing the colonies, who had been helped by the British victory.

The British Parliament had passed the Tea Act of 1773. This law placed a tax on tea coming into the colonies. Earlier,

Along with the Tea Act, the colonists were also upset with the Stamp Act. Documents, some books, and even playing cards had to be stamped with a special marking that cost money. Here, an angry mob is attempting to force a stamp officer to resign.

This engraving by Paul Revere shows the landing of British troops in Boston in 1768. The British did this to keep an eye on the colonists after some violence broke out over the Stamp Act of 1765.

Parliament had also passed several new taxes on such items as paper, glass, and paint. These taxes were known as the Townsend Acts of 1767. One of these had placed another tax on tea as well. None of this money would be used for the colonists' needs. Instead the funds would go to Britain.

The colonists were not about to accept this. They felt that the taxes were not right. The colonists had no elected officials to represent them in the British Parliament. There was no one to stand up for their interests.

They argued that there should be "no **taxation** without representation."

King George III and the British government saw things differently. They said that all British subjects were represented in Parliament. That included those living in the colonies.

But the colonists knew that Parliament cared little about them. For years, Britain had largely ignored the colonies.

In 1770, British troops shot and killed members of a group of protesting Americans. Patriots began calling this the Boston Massacre. This engraving of the Boston Massacre was made by Paul Revere.

The colonists rarely paid attention to British law and this usually went unpunished. Frequently taxes went uncollected as well.

For the most part, the colonists had been left to govern themselves. They elected their own officials and made their own rules. Living in America had given the colonists a taste of freedom. Now they did not want to be controlled by Britain.

Groups of colonists concerned about the taxes soon formed. They hoped to change things. The Sons of Liberty was one of these groups. There were many others as well. Meetings were held throughout the colonies. Leaders in different colonies wrote to one another. They knew that they had to stay united.

The colonists were determined to be heard. They thought of ways to protest British policies. The British government and their supporters in the colonies saw these individuals as troublemakers and lawbreakers. Yet many colonists saw them as **patriots**. They were people who loved their new land and were willing to fight for their rights there.

② No Tea for Me, Please

The colonists hoped to force Britain to lift the tea tax. Even before the Tea Act of 1773, some colonists had begun to **boycott** (refuse to buy) tea. That was because tea was also being taxed under the Townsend Acts of 1767. Giving up tea had not been easy. Tea was a popular drink in the colonies. It was as popular as soda or chewing gum is today. Can you imagine everyone in the United States giving up these treats? The same would be true for tea in the colonies.

The colonists' love of tea made a boycott especially difficult. So they tried to find ways to replace their favorite drink. Many colonial women began brewing herbal teas. They used various plants for different tastes. One popular tea was made from a plant called

Sometimes colonists liked to have a type of cookie called a biscuit with their tea. However, once the boycott started, the patriots only drank herbal tea.

New Jersey tea, also known as redroot. Grown in swampy areas, redroot has a strong flavor. The local American Indians had drunk it for years.

New Jersey tea, also known as redroot

The patriots liked the idea of local brews. They encouraged people to drink them. Some colonial doctors helped with this. They claimed that drinking British tea was unhealthy. Some said it would cause nervousness and sickness. Others argued that it could even lead to an early death. Much of this was not true. However, these doctors' claims gave colonists two reasons to boycott tea. They did it because they thought it would improve their health and for the good of the colony.

I MUST ADMIT, I MISS THE ENGLISH TEA.

THIS HERBAL TEA ISN'T SO BAD. I BET IT WOULD TASTE GREAT WITH MY FAVORITE DOG FOODS.

MAX

3 The Dartmouth Arrives

T he colonists had protested the Townsend Acts and enjoyed a small victory. Britain removed all the taxes except the one on tea. For a time, the colonists felt better. Though the tea boycott continued, it was not strongly followed. Some colonists only drank herbal tea. But others still drank tea from Britain.

However, the new Tea Act of 1773 again made the colonists furious. It said that the British East India

This political cartoon shows an American Indian predicting that the conflict over the Tea Act would lead to war between the colonies and Britain.

Company could sell its tea in America for half price. This was a threat to American tea traders, who had to sell their tea at regular price. On top of this, the colonists had to pay the usual tax on the British tea. Now the patriots became even more determined than ever. They would keep tea from Britain out of the colonies. All British ships carrying it were to be turned back.

The colonists' determination was soon put to the test. On November 28, 1773, the *Dartmouth* sailed into Boston Harbor. It was the first ship to arrive from Britain with a **cargo** of tea.

The patriots knew that they had to act quickly. First they spoke with the colony's tea **merchants**. These men worked for the British East India Company that sent the tea. The patriots asked the merchants to turn the ship around. They wanted the *Dartmouth* to go back to Britain. But the

Patriots were not only in Boston. People all over the colonies were angry at the British. Here, a New York barber refuses to cut the hair of a British man.

merchants refused. Their loyalty was with Britain. They made their living selling tea.

The Old South Meeting House had always been a favorite place for people to discuss issues.

Now the patriots called for a general meeting to see how people felt. On November 29, messengers on horseback were sent out to alert colonists in the surrounding areas. These men rode at top speed. They carried letters urging everyone to come to the meeting the next morning.

By 9:00 A.M. on November 30, a crowd of about five thousand had gathered. Boston's Old South Meeting House overflowed with people. Everyone there had strong feelings. They were firmly against paying the tea tax.

John Hancock inspired the crowd in the Old South Meeting House.

John Hancock led the meeting. He was a wealthy Boston merchant and an active patriot. Samuel Adams, another patriot, was there too. Adams stressed that the tea must not be allowed to leave the ship. The crowd agreed.

The colonists knew that they had to be careful. They did not want to be tricked by the tea merchants. They feared that the merchants might try to secretly unload the tea chests. Once the shipment was on land, the tax had to be paid.

So the patriots had **volunteers** guard the ship. A force of twenty-five men soon boarded the *Dartmouth*. They carried guns called **muskets** and worked in shifts. That way the ship was guarded around the clock.

The patriots also printed up posters. These warned everyone not to try to unload the ship's cargo. Anyone who did would face an angry mob.

WHO'S THAT FELLA NEXT TO YOU?

THAT'S HENRY KNOX. HE'D LATER SERVE UNDER GEORGE WASHINGTON IN THE AMERICAN REVOLUTION.

4 Remaining Determined

The local tea merchants were very upset. The colonists' boycott had cost them money.

So the merchants went to see the governor of the Massachusetts colony. That was a man named Thomas Hutchinson. As the colony's governor, Hutchinson was an official of the British government. He was also quite disliked among many of the colonists.

The governor issued a public order to the colony. He demanded that the tea boycott stop. Hutchinson also wanted no further meetings held. The patriots ignored Hutchinson. They were not about to let him tell them what to do.

Yet not everyone in the colony was a patriot. Some were still fiercely loyal to Britain and King George III. These people were called Loyalists or Tories. Tensions between the patriots and the Loyalists grew. The tea merchants became fearful. They did not want to be harmed or have their property destroyed. Still, at times, violence broke out. A tea merchant

King George III felt that he should be able to tax the colonies however he wanted to.

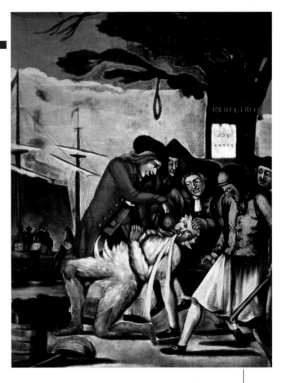

This cartoon shows colonists pouring tea down a tax collector's throat. The colonists have covered him in tar and feathers. In the background, men dump tea from a ship.

named Richard Clarke became a victim of the violence.

The patriots had wanted Clarke to quit his job. That meant he would no longer work as a merchant for the British East India Company. Clarke refused and paid a high price for it. An angry mob damaged his store. Other merchants were threatened too.

Members of the patriot group the Sons of Liberty often met at the Green Dragon Tavern.

The patriots were active in Virginia too. Here, a colonist loyal to Britain is forced to sign an anti-British document. If he refused, he would be covered in hot tar and then have feathers stuck to him.

Through it all, the colonies remained united. Patriots in the cities of New York and Philadelphia followed the lead of those in Boston. No ships carrying tea from England entered their ports. In Philadelphia, all the tea merchants resigned. Those in the New York colony did the same.

Despite the distance between the different colonies, the patriots stayed in close touch. Messengers rode back and forth bringing news. They galloped through rainstorms and sleet. Sometimes they were on the road for days. But they knew they had an important job to do.

Patriots in Philadelphia and New York cheered on the Boston colonists. They urged them to stay strong. The patriots in Boston would need both strength and courage. On December 7, two more British ships arrived in port. Both carried tea shipments. These were the *Eleanor* and the *Beaver*. Soon, the patriots would have to make a very hard decision: What should they do about all these British tea ships?

5 A Tough Decision

Things grew worse in Boston. British law called for a tax on any tea brought into the harbor by ship. December 16 was the last day before the tax was due.

If the colonists did not act, the tea owners would pay the tax. Then, British customs officers would take the tea off the ships. They would use force if necessary. After that, the tea merchants would sell the tea. They would charge their customers tax to make up for the tax they paid Britain.

THE COLONISTS WERE DETERMINED NOT TO PAY THE TEA TAX.

THERE SURE ARE LOTS OF PEOPLE HERE.

The patriots knew that not all the colonists supported the boycott. Some were still loyal to Britain. Others just wanted a good cup of tea. They were willing to pay the British tax.

The patriots did not have very much time left. They had to come up with an answer quickly. A meeting was called for December 16.

That day, colonists poured into Boston. They could be seen coming for miles. The large number of people could not even fit into the Old South Meeting House.

The patriots had asked a man named Francis Rotch to be there. He was the son of the *Dartmouth*'s owner. The elder Rotch had been asked to send his ship back to Britain. However, the British customs officers would not allow the ship to leave until the tax was paid.

The colonists at the meeting sent Francis Rotch to see Governor Hutchinson. He asked the governor if his father's ship could set sail. The governor refused. Also, the British Royal Navy warships *Active* and *Kingfisher* were under orders to prevent any tea ships from leaving without permission.

The pulpit was a place from which a person could speak at the Old South Meeting House.

At that point, the patriots faced a tough decision. For weeks, some of them had met in secret. They discussed throwing the tea overboard. However, they tried to avoid breaking the law. Now, they felt that they had few choices left. That night they would turn Boston's harbor into one big teapot.

Francis Rotch (played here by a modern man) told the patriots that the governor had refused to let the *Dartmouth* set sail.

6 The Night of the Boston Tea Party

The patriots knew what they had to do. Yet these men were putting themselves at great risk.

British warships were anchored in the waters close by. If the British caught the patriots, things would not go well for them. They could be arrested. Some might even be shot on the spot.

Therefore, secrecy was especially important that night. After dark, the men went to their secret meeting places. There, they hurriedly tried to disguise themselves.

The men dressed like Mohawk Indians. They wrapped

The patriots grew upset during the meeting at the Old South Meeting House. These people are pretending to be patriots from the 1700s.

A man playing Samuel Adams (top) listens to someone speak at the Old South Meeting House. He is waiting to give the signal to patriots to start preparing for the tea party if no agreement is made. Below is a portrait of the real Samuel Adams.

blankets around their shoulders and tied feathers in their hair. They carried **tomahawks** (axes) and clubs.

Then they headed for Griffin's **Wharf**. That is where the ships carrying the tea were docked. The patriots arrived in small groups. Some were very young, like fourteen-year-old Peter Slater.

Most of the men had gone down Milk Street and then on to Hutchinson Street. People heard them coming and ran to their windows. They felt that something important was about to happen. They were right.

7 Tossing Tea Into the Sea

Before long, about one hundred fifty patriots had reached the wharf. The men quickly divided into three groups. Each had a leader who had been picked beforehand.

There was no time to lose. Carrying lanterns and torches, the men boarded the ships. They were prepared to take the vessels by force. But as it turned out, that was not necessary. The British crews did not resist.

Once on board, the men opened the hatches. They soon found what they were looking for. The cargo area was filled with chests of tea.

Each chest weighed about three hundred pounds. The men pulled

Men had to join together to toss the heavy tea chests into the sea.

the heavy wooden chests up to the deck. It was tiring work and their arms ached. Yet no one stopped to rest. Fifteen-year-old Joshua Wyeth would later say, "I never worked harder in my life."

The patriots split the tea chests open with their tomahawks. Then they heaved the tea into the water. The men smashed the empty chests too. They threw the wood pieces overboard as well.

The colonists used tomahawks or hatchets (axes) to split open the tea chests.

The clang of the Mohawks' tomahawks rang out in the night. The sound drew a crowd to the wharf. Over a thousand people left their homes to see what was going on.

It took about three hours to finish the job. In all, 342 chests of tea were ruined. No other damage was done to the ship.

This was very important to the men. They saw themselves as patriots, not criminals. They had only come to destroy the tea. The crew and other

This is one of the actual tea chests from the Boston Tea Party. Only two are known to exist.

People on Griffin's Wharf watched and cheered as the disguised colonists rowed off to toss the tea into the harbor.

cargo were not touched. Before going, they even swept the decks clean.

On the way home, some of the patriots passed a house where a British admiral was visiting. He had seen everything from the window.

When the admiral heard the "Mohawks" outside, he called out to them. (The British knew the Mohawks were really colonists.) He told the men that they would pay for what they had done. It was their first warning of things to come.

The patriots knew that the British would be angry. Still, they did not know just how

important their tea party was. Yet, after that night the colonies would never be the same. How would the British show their anger? Should the colonists be preparing for war? Only the coming months would give the colonists the answers they needed.

8 Afterward

News of the Boston Tea Party spread quickly. Colonists in New York and Philadelphia admired the Boston patriots' bravery. People in other colonies felt the same way. As it turned out, the Boston colonists had set an example. Soon there were other tea parties in different colonies.

King George III and Parliament were not happy. They were determined to punish the Boston colonists. To do so, Parliament passed the Boston Port Act. As of June 1, 1774, Boston Harbor was closed. No ships could go in or out until the destroyed tea was paid for.

This hurt the Massachusetts colonists. Many of them made their living through shipping. Nevertheless, the colonists voted against paying for the ruined tea.

Britain was not about to give up either. Still more laws were passed to limit

Waving his axe, an actor portraying a tea tosser returns from Boston Harbor.

the Massachusetts colonists' freedom. Now these colonists could no longer elect their own officials. Britain appointed them instead. Public meetings were outlawed too. A law called the Quartering Act was especially hard on the colonists. According to this act, British soldiers could be sheltered anywhere their officers chose. This included the colonists' homes.

Many of the colonists in Massachusetts were angry. They even called these unfair laws the Intolerable Acts. This meant that the colonists mostly found these laws impossible to accept.

> ## To the Public.
>
> THE long expected TEA SHIP arrived laft night at Sandy-Hook, but the pilot would not bring up the Captain till the fenfe of the city was known. The committee were immediately informed of her arrival, and that the Captain folicits for liberty to come up to provide neceffaries for his return. The fhip to remain at Sandy-Hook. The committee conceiving it to be the fenfe of the city that he fhould have fuch liberty, fignified it to the Gentleman who is to fupply him with provifions, and other neceffaries. Advice of this was immediately difpatched to the Captain; and whenever he comes up, care will be taken that he does not enter at the cuftom-houfe, and that no time be loft in difpatching him.
>
> New-York, April 19, 1774.

This notice from April 19, 1774 describes how a tea ship was prevented from landing in New York in 1774.

Leaders in other colonies grew angry as well. They saw what Britain was doing to the Massachusetts colonists. They wondered if their colony would be next.

They decided to meet in Philadelphia in September 1774. This gathering

This cartoon shows a man in flames who represents America. British men are making the flames rise with laws like the Boston Port Bill (which became the Boston Port Act), while colonists are trying to put the flames out. In front of the man representing America is a fallen tea kettle.

The First Continental Congress met in Carpenter's Hall in Philadelphia.

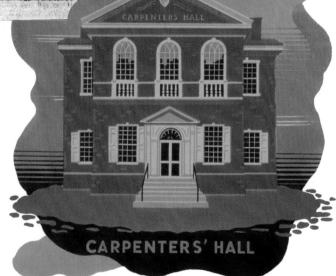

became known as the First Continental Congress. All the colonies sent men to represent them except Georgia. However, this southern colony agreed in advance to any decisions the Congress made.

Through the First Continental Congress, the colonists let Britain know where they stood. The colonists refused to obey unfair laws. They would not pay unfair taxes either. The Congress also called for a boycott of British goods.

Massachusetts soldiers were called minutemen. They were ready to fight the British army in a minute's notice if they needed to.

The colonists did not know what King George III and Parliament would do next. But they feared the worst. They knew that Britain might use its army against them. If that happened, the colonists were ready to fight back. They felt that the freedom and liberty they were used to were now at stake.

9 Fighting Back

The colonists had to act quickly. They needed to put together an army. Most of these men had never been soldiers before. They were farmers, laborers, and merchants. Many were teenagers. A few were grandfathers.

Now, after a full day's work, they did military drills. In Massachusetts, the men formed **militias**. They called themselves Minutemen. They were ready and willing to fight on a minute's notice.

The colonists desperately needed weapons as well. They soon collected every available musket and a good supply of gunpowder. They stored these in Concord—a town near Boston.

The British were also prepared to fight. British General Thomas Gage was the new governor of the Massachusetts colony. Gage had spies working for him. They told him about the colonists' stored weapons at Concord. He also learned that Samuel Adams and John Hancock were hiding in Lexington—just miles from Concord. These men had become very important patriot leaders. Gage hoped to catch them.

Colonists prepare to defend themselves by making weapons.

In April 1775, Gage made his move. He sent seven hundred soldiers to Lexington to arrest Adams and Hancock. From there, the soldiers were to go on to Concord to seize the weapons. The British did not think highly of the colonists' poorly trained militias. They felt certain of success.

However, the patriots had their own spies. They learned about Gage's plan. Then the colonists sprang into action.

Gage's soldiers were to reach Lexington on April 19. But on the night of April 18, a patriot named Paul Revere made his famous midnight ride. He rode through the countryside at top speed, warning the colonists that the British were coming. Paul Revere reached Samuel Adams

Paul Revere was not the only one that tried to warn people of the approaching British. William Dawes also rode his horse to raise the alarm.

and John Hancock before Gage's soldiers did. The pair escaped in time.

When the British arrived in Lexington, the Minutemen were waiting for them. Gage's soldiers far outnumbered the patriots. But the Minutemen were not about to run and hide. They bravely faced their enemy.

Shots rang out. No one is sure which side fired first. However, before it was over, eight Minutemen were dead. About ten more were wounded.

The Minutemen lost the Battle of Lexington. The shot that started the battle was called "the shot heard round the world." This was because the world's nations took notice when the American Revolution started.

From Lexington, the British troops went on to Concord. Fighting broke out there as well. Both sides lost men.

Luckily, the British were unable to complete their mission. Most of the weapons hidden at Concord had already been moved. The British were only able to destroy a small part of the colonists' supply.

Then the British began their march back to Boston. At that point, they thought the fighting was over. They did not count on what happened next.

The Minutemen and the British clashed at Concord Bridge.

Though the British thought they were alone, they were not. The Minutemen had been quietly trailing them. Suddenly, the British soldiers heard shots. The Minutemen had begun firing at them from behind trees, barns, and fences.

The British could not see their enemy. They did not know where the bullets were coming from. Hopelessly, they tried to fire back. But the Minutemen had the upper hand. By the time they reached Boston, the British had lost about two hundred fifty men.

The fighting at Lexington and Concord changed life in the colonies forever. The famous poet Ralph Waldo Emerson later wrote about that day. He described the patriots as firing "the shot heard round the world." These battles marked the start of a long and difficult war. The American Revolution had begun.

10 Heading Home

The Boston Tea Party was an extremely important event in American history. It proved to be much more than just an act of protest. Britain's harsh reaction to it caused the colonists to unite. They saw how much freedom meant to them. They were willing to fight and die for it.

When the American Revolution was over, the colonies were an independent nation. In time, that nation grew into one of the world's most powerful countries—the United States of America. Yet it all began with the Boston Tea Party.

Today, people celebrate the Boston Tea Party by tossing fake chests of tea into Boston Harbor.

Of course, the colonists taking part in that event never imagined its importance. They were simply demanding fair treatment. It just shows what can happen when people stand up for what they believe in.

THANKS FOR HELPING WITH THE TEA PARTY, MAX.

YOU CAN ALWAYS COUNT ON ME!

Max and I really liked being at the Boston Tea Party. But now it is time to go. It was great traveling with you. Time travel is always more fun when we do it with friends. To the time machine!

This sketch shows the events leading up to the American Revolution. The Boston Tea Party can be seen at the bottom left.

What Ever Happened To . . .

While time traveling, Max and I always meet some interesting people. Here is what became of a few of them from Boston:

SAMUEL ADAMS

Samuel Adams was a leader in the colonists' fight for independence. He helped plan the Boston Tea Party. Adams was later a signer of the Declaration of Independence. He remained active in government for the rest of his life. Samuel Adams served as governor of Massachusetts from 1793 to 1798. He died in 1803.

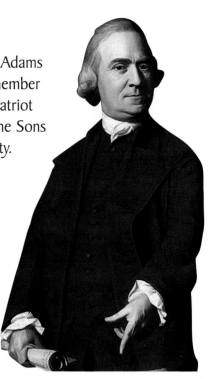

Samuel Adams was a member of the patriot group the Sons of Liberty.

JOHN HANCOCK

John Hancock, like Samuel Adams, helped the colonies win their independence. Hancock was one of the wealthiest men in Boston. Yet he risked it all for freedom. Hancock served in the Continental Congress and signed the Declaration of Independence as well. His large signature on this document has become famous.

John Hancock served in the Continental Congress and was the first to sign the Declaration of Independence.

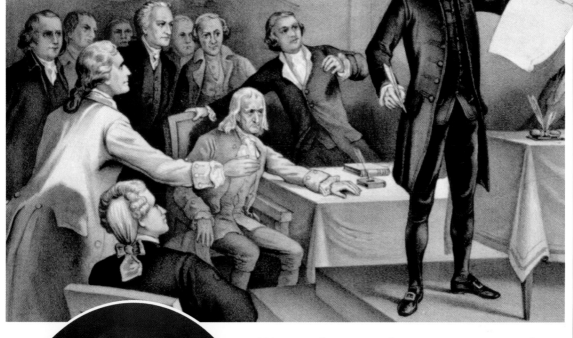

Hancock served as governor of Massachusetts until 1793. He died on October 8, 1793.

PAUL REVERE

Like the other men noted here, Paul Revere was a great patriot. In his early years, Revere had been an outstanding **silversmith** (a person who makes things from silver). Then after serving as a

Paul Revere was a silversmith. He made many beautiful objects from silver.

lieutenant colonel during the American Revolution, Revere opened the nation's first copper rolling mill. It produced goods made from copper for the new Massachusetts State House. Revere started the mill so that the United States would not have to import copper goods from Britain. Paul Revere died in 1818 at the age of eighty-three.

Paul Revere's house in Boston is a historic site and can be visited today.

Farewell Fellow Explorer,

I just wanted to take a moment to tell you a little about the real "Max and me." I am a children's book author and Max is a small, fluffy, white dog. I almost named him Marshmallow because of how he looked. However, he seems to think he's human—so only a more dignified name would do. Max also seems to think that he is a large, powerful dog. He fearlessly chases after much larger dogs in the neighborhood. Max was thrilled when the artist for this book drew him as a dog several times his size. He felt that someone in the art world had finally captured his true spirit.

In real life, Max is quite a traveler. I have taken him to nearly every state while doing research for different books. We live in Florida so when we go north I have to pack a sweater for him. When we were in Oregon it rained and I was glad I brought his raincoat. None of this gear is necessary when time traveling. My "take-off" spot is the computer station and as always Max sits faithfully by my side.

Best Wishes,
Elaine & Max
(a small dog with big dreams)

Timeline

1767 The Townsend Acts are passed taxing a number of household items used by the colonists.

1773 **November 28**—The *Dartmouth* sails into Boston Harbor.

November 29—Messengers leave the Boston colony to call for a general meeting.

November 30—Meeting held in Boston with over five thousand colonists attending.

December 7—The *Eleanor* and the *Beaver* arrive in Boston—both ships are carrying tea shipments.

December 16 (day)—Meeting held in Boston; Francis Rotch speaks to the group.

(evening)—The Boston Tea Party takes place.

1774 **June 1**—The British close Boston Harbor.

September—The First Continental Congress is held.

1775 **April 18**—Paul Revere makes his famous midnight ride.

April 19—The battles at Lexington and Concord are fought.

1793 John Hancock dies.

1803 Samuel Adams dies.

1818 Paul Revere dies.

Words to Know

boycott—To refuse to buy something.

cargo—Goods carried by a ship.

colony—A group of people who settle in a new land.

merchant—Someone who sells goods.

militia—A group of citizens trained to fight in an emergency.

musket—A type of gun used before there were rifles.

Parliament—A form of government in Britain in which people are elected to office. They pass laws to govern the nation.

patriot—A person who loves his or her country.

patriotic—Strongly loving one's country.

taxation—Money that must be paid by people to support their government.

volunteer—Offering to do a job or task without pay.

wharf—A dock where boats can load and unload.

Further Reading

Burgan, Michael. *The Boston Tea Party*. Minneapolis: Compass Point Books, 2001.

Dolan, Edward. *The Boston Tea Party*. New York: Benchmark Books, 2002.

Edwards, Pamela Duncan. *Boston Tea Party*. New York: Putnam, 2001.

Fradin, Dennis Brindell. *Let It Begin Here!: Lexington & Concord: First Battles of the American Revolution*. New York: Walker & Company, 2005.

Hossell, Karen Price. *The Boston Tea Party*. Chicago: Heinemann Library, 2003.

Krensky, Stephen. *Paul Revere's Midnight Ride*. New York: HarperCollins, 2002.

Stuart, Murray. *Eyewitness: American Revolution*. New York: DK Publishing, 2002.

Web Sites

The Boston Tea Party Ship & Museum.

<http://www.bostonteapartyship.com/overview.asp>

Visit the site of the museum that recreates the Boston Tea Party for visitors. Don't miss the replicas of the ships.

The Declaration of Independence.

<http://www.ushistory.org/declaration>

Check out this Web site to learn about the Declaration of Independence and those who signed it.

The Paul Revere House.

<http://www.paulreverehouse.org>

This site tells everything you'd want to know about the famous patriot Paul Revere. He played an active part in the Boston Tea Party and much more.

Index